Art Media Series

Creating with Space and Construction

Lothar Kampmann

 Van Nostrand Reinhold Company/New York

Illustrations
The illustrations in the first part of the book are by students of the Ruhr Teachers' Training College, Dortmund Section, and by the author. The illustrations in the Appendix are from the archives of the Department of Art and Craft Education of the Ruhr Teachers' Training College, Dortmund Section. A further source was the Overberg School, Recklinghausen.

Photographs: Wilhelm Homann, Recklinghausen (69); Prestel Verlag, Munich (1); Städtische Kunsthalle, Mannheim (1).

Sponsored by the Günther Wagner Pelikan-Werke, Hanover; and Koh-I-Nor, Inc., 100 North Street, Bergen, New Jersey 08804.

German edition © 1971 by Otto Maier Verlag, Ravensburg, Germany.

English translation Copyright ©1973 by Evans Brothers Limited.

Library of Congress Catalog Card Number 72—2791
ISBN 0—442—24248—4

Printed in Italy

Published in the United States of America, 1973, by Van Nostrand Reinhold Company, a Division of Litton Educational Publishing, Inc., 450 West 33rd Street, New York, N.Y. 10001.

16 15 14 13 12 11 10 9 8 7 6 5 4 3 2 1

Experiencing space

All experience is three-dimensional and everything which is three-dimensional — that is, all space — is full of experience. We experience space and fill it with life. Being three-dimensional, we ourselves form spaces within other spaces. We can, of course, continue this line of thought infinitely, for these other spaces are only part of what we call 'outer space', which, vast though it may be, is tiny compared with the boundless, all-consuming space which our minds and senses are incapable of grasping.

We experience space by passing or looking through it; or, alternatively, by embracing or encircling it. We can measure space and, if this is impossible, the mind creates limits. We are even aware of space when our eyes are closed. Its infinity frightens us, but our knowledge of how to measure and limit it affords us security.

There is nothing in the world which does not in some way occupy space or, by its very position, define space. Without an elementary knowledge of the nature of space and three-dimensionality we would be completely lost. Our hands and eyes would make no sense of the world.

We live in space; it is at our disposal. We use it; we fill and empty it; yet we do not *know* space. We are not even amazed at its existence. In order to be able to experience the world fully, we must try to recognize the character of different types of space and their relationships to each other. Only then is it possible for us properly to find our way about within space.

By holding a stone in our hand we can learn certain basic things about space — things which are vital to ourselves and all living things, to plants, objects and all forms of construction. The stone held in the hand shows us three fundamentals concerning space.

1. The stone. It embraces a space taken up by itself, which stretches to the limit of its volume—its outer 'skin'. It is compact.

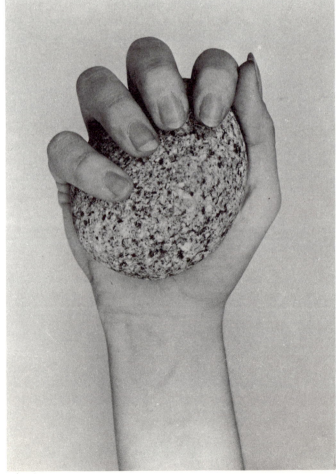

2. The hand. It encloses the stone like the bars of a prison cell; the prisoner can look out, but cannot escape. It is encircled and enclosed.

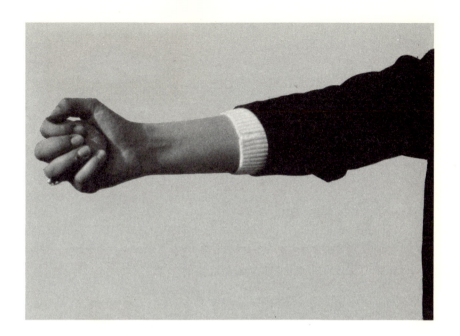

3. Hand, arm and stone reach out into unlimited space. Thus they encounter the depth and expansion of space. They penetrate and pass through it.

We can attach symbols to these various types of space. We can represent volumetric, compact space by a sphere. Encircled, enclosed space, which can contain corporeal objects but is not necessarily corporeal itself, can be represented by a cage. And the skeleton can act as a symbol for broken space, which we experience through its direction, thereby forming an abstract concept of its volume.

We cannot present space itself. It will always be a space filled with spatial structures, or spatial structures representing space itself. It will always be a limited space; an interior or exterior; something containing space or contained by space.

The world around us provides an abundant variety of examples.

A beetle in a box, the box in a boy's hand, the boy in a room, the room in an apartment, the apartment in a house, the house in a town. And so it goes on. Each space is contained within another space. For the beetle the box is the space; for the boy it is the room. Our knowledge of the world is graded according to space. For a baby, space is limited to the cradle. For a child of two it is a room and all the objects contained within that room. For older children and adults the room is experienced as a space within a house—interior and exterior are differentiated. In this way our experience grows until we reach the conclusion that our world, and the spaces contained within it, is one of many worlds contained within even vaster spaces.

a

b

c

The earth seen from the moon.

Photograph: USIS/NASA.
This was taken using a lens made by Carl
Zeiss, Oberkochen/Württ.

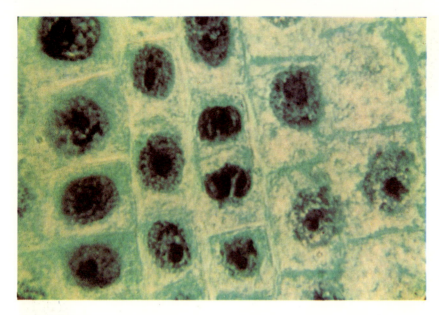

Cell division, telophase.
Photograph: V-Dia.

Just as important as the realization of the infinity of outer space is the realization of the infinity of inner space. We know about human cells, about the nuclei in the cells and the chromosomes within the nuclei; we have also recognized that matter is made up of molecules, which further contain atoms, within which there are protons and neutrons. Space is indeed something miraculous. It embraces all that is immeasurably small and all that is immeasurably vast.

We stand between the two and can experience and comprehend both because we have the ability to think as well as to see, touch and feel. To us we represent the centre of space; yet we must remember that we are not the only 'centres'; for every object can be the centre of space and can take on relationships to other objects and spaces.

Spaces can interconnect, penetrate, enclose and intersect each other.

The size and extent of space are always relative. If we hold a small mushroom in our hand, it seems tiny to us. For the even smaller worm in the mushroom, which might spend its whole life eating through it, it represents the immeasurability of space. Since we possess the means to see, touch, feel, move and think, we should use these powers to increase our knowledge of space.

Compact space

Earlier we represented this type of space by a sphere. For many reasons the sphere gives us an idea of both the beginning and the end of compact space. The nucleus of the ovum—the beginning of human life—is spherical, and so too is the vast volumetric body upon which human life depends—the earth. Shape, which is determined by substance and function, is a criterion of space. All substance takes on its own distinctive shape without changing its given volume. Volume is measured by finding out the amount of space which it displaces.

Let us take a lump of clay, for example. We measure its volume by placing it in a beaker of water and measuring the amount of water displaced.

As clay can be moulded into different shapes, we can easily mould it into a sphere—that is, a ball. We can now see that the ball of clay occupies the same space as the unshaped lump. Thus we can show that the volume is not dependent on shape.

If you roll the clay ball into the shape of a rod, the length of the new shape points out space in one direction.

Now shape the rod into a coil; it will then embrace a new shape.

Or make the clay ball into a thin slab. The latitudinal expansion of the same quantity of clay now points out the space above it.

If you now bend the edges of the slab upwards, you produce a dish which holds space.

In each of these cases the volume of the clay has remained the same, despite the various shapes which it has taken on. Of course it would be difficult to discuss volume in this way with solid objects which cannot be moulded into different shapes.

Let us continue to look at volumetric space—that is, the space of which an object consists. The sphere is the ideal shape, as with the least surface it contains the greatest volume. But the true sphere only exists in mathematical calculation. The roundest pebble or insect egg is not perfectly spherical. All the spherical shapes on this earth are in some way 'deformed'.

With bird's eggs the deformation is the apex.

With walnuts, horse chestnuts and acorns there is also a flattening towards the base.

The characteristic shape of pears, certain pumpkins and quince is determined by the 'neck'.

Apples have conical hollows at both poles.

Plums and peaches have deep grooves.

As well as these deformations of the spherical shape, we also find less fundamental deformations of the surface, which may be pitted or bumpy, as is the case with the lemon.

Or almost geometrically ordered and indented, as is the case with the pineapple.

Pebbles which are composed of stratified rock consist of rings of varying depth; they are therefore 'deformed', yet in principle they remain spherical.

By remodelling spherical shapes we gain insight into all the various shapes which mass can assume. All these structures have volume — and it is their volume that we are interested in. The structures in question can, of course, constantly take on new spatial functions. Volumetric space is the foremost of all spatial concepts.

Let us imagine a medium-sized clay ball, which we can reshape or 'damage'. By cutting the clay we could produce a cube or a pyramid, or we could press the clay into the shape of a bowl. On the other hand, we could create the bowl shape by cutting into the sphere, and the cube or pyramid by banging the clay against a solid object. In the one instance we would be reshaping the mass without there being any loss of that mass; in the other instance we would be damaging the mass and there would be a resultant loss of mass. In this way spherical objects could be turned into any shape. This is a starting point for creative activity and will be discussed more fully later.

There are certain ways by which we can find out how large the space contained by a compact object is. One method has already been mentioned: that of displacement (see page 9). The other methods are familiar to us in everyday life. We can indicate with our hands how wide, how high and how deep an object is.

Or we can copy the tailor taking our measurements for a suit.

He puts his tape measure around the chest or waist because he cannot measure through them. Children can use the same method to measure a tree trunk.

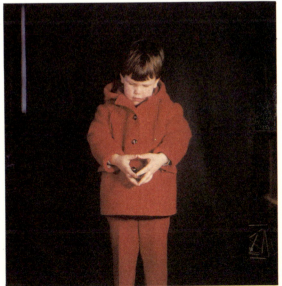

Or to show each other how big the apples in their garden were this year.

15

Enclosed, encircled or latticed space.

Having looked at the space which objects *consist of,* we now turn to the space *taken up* by objects. This means that we must take into consideration all hollow objects, such as bowls, dishes, jugs and bottles. These enclose space, but usually in such a way that a con-nexion remains between the inner and the outer space. Hollow bodies can, of course, be filled, and their content capacity is measured by the quantity of any particular substance which they are capable of holding. This also applies to all boxes, crates, cartons and tins.

All types of lattices or cages also form 'hollow spaces', and ordinary kitchen utensils such as the strainer come into this category. The capacity of objects such as these cannot, however, be measured by filling them and then pouring the content out again. In this case inner and outer space are in contact on all sides.

The space contained within such utensils is totally independent of the amount of material which goes to make up the lattice or cage. The fact that a cup is made of bone china or thick plastic does not necessarily affect its inner or 'hollow' space.

But there are exceptions. When you blow up a balloon, for example, its inner space expands although the mass of the balloon itself remains the same. In this case, however, there is no permanent connexion between inner and outer space.

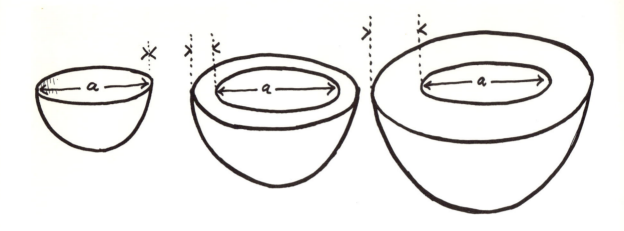

When we wanted to express the compact space in pictorial terms, the mass of the inner space served as a medium. With the hollow space, however, the wall or lattice enclosing the space takes over this function. The hollow space and the lattice space are very closely related to each other—the one can be transformed into the other.

The walls of a hollow sphere, bowl or box need only be perforated and the object in question takes on the function of a lattice or sieve. Alternatively, if the distance between the individual bars of a lattice construction is very small, one could easily imagine that it were a box.

Liana in a tropical rain forest.
Photograph: V-Dia.

In the context of the hollow shape and lattice construction we must also mention the spiral, although this also bears great similarity to the 'traversed space' discussed in the following section. An example of this is the liana. Taking a further example from everyday life, the knitted stocking is also based on the same principle. In both cases a hollow space is enclosed. Some forms of pottery also provide an excellent illustration. Containers are made simply by building up a spiral.

Straw bee-hives are made by using the same principle.

Finally, we must mention the tube, which also comes under the general heading of hollow spaces, though a tube—like the latticed space—is not a container.

In the practical sections of the book, therefore, we shall be dealing with hollow bodies, boxes, lattices, tubes and spirals.

The traversed space

Here we are talking of structures which reach out into a space and therefore penetrate it. They create the illusion of enclosing a space by using the space which surrounds them. Trees are a good example of this; *optically* their branches enclose space. In this way a relatively small mass can take up a large space. All spiny objects come under this category.

If we remove all the spines except six from the object below, we are able to detach the height, length and width of a new space from the surrounding space. As the spiny object becomes more complex, it becomes easier to see what kind of spatial shape the structure is taking up.

The difference can be seen clearly if you compare a tree which has shed all its leaves with one which is still densely covered with leaves.

The existence of the occupied space becomes clearer as the object reaching out into space becomes denser. In order to illustrate the traversed space pictorially, we shall be looking at the skeleton constructon later in the book.

Combined living-room and study.
Photograph: Behr Möbel.

Spatial arrangement and composition.

So far we have only considered various types of space as separate entities, whereas in reality all spaces exist in relation to one another. This introduces the problem of spatial composition. Things can stand, lie, hang, recline and even float in space.

Spatial arrangement is more complex than surface arrangement, for here one has to deal with a top, bottom, front and back, as well as all the resultant variations. Spatial arrangement is a basic problem with regard to sculptural construction. Our everyday environment illustrates the importance of co-ordination; just think of the difference between a well-arranged room and one which is untidily filled with all sorts of objects. If we consider the ways in which we use space in our everyday lives, we can see that spatial arrangement is extremely important to all human activity.

TWA Terminal, Kennedy Airport, New York.
Photograph: Oswald W. Grube.

23

Three-dimensional construction

The *arrangements* depicted in the two-dimensional field of painting and drawing can also be used three-dimensionally, that is, spatially. All forms of construction— sculptures, models, etc.—raise spatial problems, because everything takes place in space, everything *is* space in so far as it either encloses or occupies space. And in every case space takes on a particular shape; if this were not so, space would be incomprehensible to us. It follows that problems of space and problems of shape are in some way interdependent. The shape of a three-dimensional object is usually governed by its function, or by the method in which it was created; function and method are further governed by the material of which the particular object is made.

The shape of any container, machine or room is, therefore, dependent on its particular function. On the other hand, the shape of a pebble, crystal or piece of clay presents us with guidelines as to the conditions under which this particular shape was created.

All variations of spatial shape are based on the following:

1. the compact, volumetric space; here mass may be transformed either without any resultant loss of mass, or by adding or removing mass;
2. the enclosed space with distinct borders; all hollow spaces come into this category, whether they are separated from their surrounding space by real partitions or optically by 'lattices';
3. the space enclosed by structures reaching out and penetrating their surrounding space; this is best expressed by skeleton structures.

The following pages offer suggestions for dealing with the three above variations. It will be seen that they are often similar to each other and even overlap.

The compact, volumetric space—the mass

There are three ways in which it is possible to deal structurally with the compact space:

1. If the material is of a consistency which is amenable to moulding, we can transform the material by all forms of stretching, pulling, etc. This is possible with clay, wax, papier-mâché and Plasticine, and in a more general way with sand and all substances which can become modelling materials by adding adhesives or pastes.

2. We can 'damage' the original compact mass by removing parts of it, for example by scraping or cutting bits off, or by drilling holes into it. This will result in a loss of volume and forms a method of transforming solid materials such as wood, plaster of Paris, brick.

3. We can add smaller quantities (or objects) to larger structures in order to create new shapes. It will be seen that addition and removal complement each other. This method of constructing a spatial object is not dependent on any particular material.

Modelling

Creating three-dimensional structures from plastic materials amounts basically to modelling. In fact, with plastic materials everything can be modelled—compact space, the space lattice and the space skeleton. And so the plastic art of both professional sculptors and children is usually made up of a combination of these three possibilities.

But we are not concerned here with free sculpting, but with the representation of space. As a starting point we can take modelling clay or fire-clay.

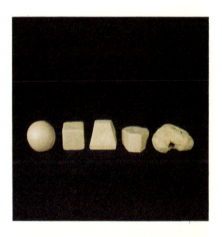

If beaten on a firm, even surface it can be transformed into whatever type of geometrical structure may be desired.

If it is pressed or beaten uniformly on all sides, the result will be the ultimate expression of compact space—the sphere.

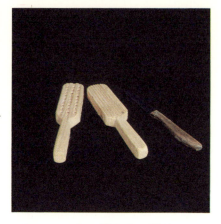

Beaters (see illustration) marked with notches and grooves can be used to shape these geometrical structures. The structures will retain their compact nature; only their outer shell will be structured. The structural aspect is, therefore, not attached artificially, but is part of the whole construction.

The addition of rolls or slabs of clay alters the outward appearance of the structures, but their compact nature remains. This is still the case even if they are indented or hollowed out in some way.

Only when the indentations or projections are of extreme proportions is the general character altered, for only then do the structures lose their compact nature. An interesting form of creative teaching could be the development of unshaped slabs of modelling clay into a variety of

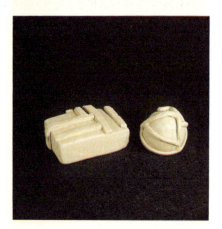

compact structures within the bounds of our definition of compact space.

Different techniques have to be applied when we are dealing with wooden blocks, plaster of Paris, bricks or fired blocks of clay. Each material has its own special character and must be treated accordingly. However, what applied to mouldable materials generally also applies here. The whole range of three-dimensional shapes can be developed—from the compact, solid shape through to the complete 'deformation'. The methods for achieving this have already been discussed (see page 25). Spatial objects made of solid materials should be worked particularly carefully in order to bring out their surface qualities— smoothness, exact edges, etc. In the same way, as with plastic materials, it would also be a useful exercise to attempt to create a good shape with solid materials— that is, something which is pleasant to touch and which is aesthetically pleasing. Both negative and positive shapes can, of course, be created.

Solid materials should be treated as 'plastically' as possible; that is, in a volumetric, compact way. At the same time, however, solid, resistant mass tends to diverge from its true character. Extreme 'deformations' will again lead to lattice and skeleton structures.

The experience gained from dealing creatively with mass and space are the basis for a feeling for form, which again is the basis for sculpture. There is scope for variation by arranging spatial objects in rows or by placing them on top of each other. The sum of these combined structures yields new three-dimensional constructions.

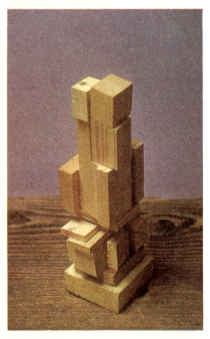

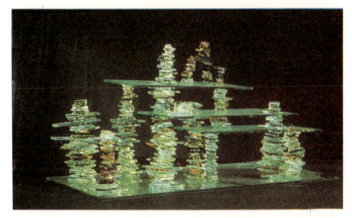

29

All types of piles and clusters come under this category; as a unit they again form compact space. The most complex structures can be made by using the simple theory of traversed space.

By assembling solid objects we are, however, leaving the field of modelling and sculpture and approaching that of building and construction.

Hollow and latticed space

Here we are, of course, dealing with the surface surrounding the inner space. And again it is pos-sible to differentiate three types of approach:

1. Boxes, bowls, cans, vases; in fact, all types of container, includ-ing tubes. All sorts of material can be used: wood, cardboard, paper, tin, fired clay and modelling clay.

2. The lattice, cage and spiral. Again, all sorts of material are possible: wood, wire, strips of strong cardboard and folded sheets of paper—even clay, which can then be fired.

3. The combination of boxes or lattices. By arranging them in a systematic way, the separate enti-ties can be piled one on top of the other or can traverse each other.

Boxes, bowls, cans, vases, etc.

Containers are characterized by a small amount of mass and a large amount of enclosed space. A great variety of materials can be used; for example, pasteboard, cardboard, wood, clay and tin.

There are also plenty of materials to be found in everyday life, and we should make use of these. The walls of these containers can be decorated with all kinds of plastic materials without interfering with the basic characteristics of the container. The container and its shape are closely interlinked, so if you want to create new containers, you first have to create new shapes. And this can be a rewarding exercise.

Etruscan vase, c. 700 B.C.
From *Kerimisches Gestalten* by Benno Geiger. By kind permission of Paul Haupt Verlag, Berne.

The strength of the walls is unimportant so long as they do in fact form a 'container'. Any form of break in the 'wall' dividing the inner space from the outer space brings the structure a little further in the direction of latticed space.

Lattice, cage, spiral

Here the wall is definitely broken. In fact, inner and outer space are only divided *optically*. With containers the strength of the walls was of little importance—it was the shape that mattered. Here a third factor has to be considered— the structure of the lattice. This creates a wealth of new possibilities.

In addition to the simple vertical- horizontal or diagonal forms, all types of lattice which are graphically effective can be created.

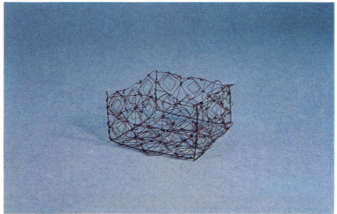

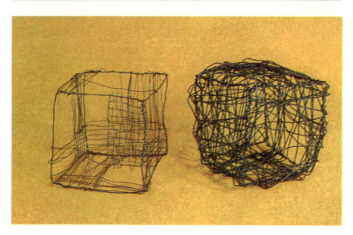

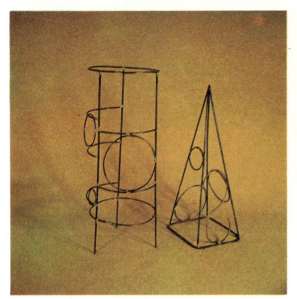

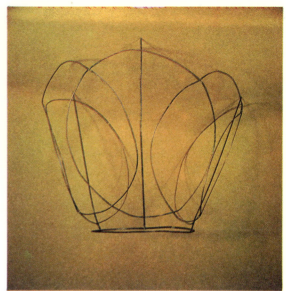

We can let the imagination run free. Obviously wire, wood and clay are the ideal materials for space lattices. But cellular concrete can also be recommended; it can easily be cut, sawn or scraped.

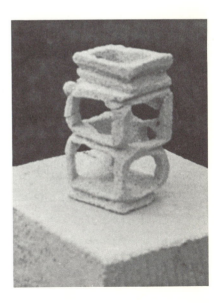

Another obvious possibility is the use of strong folded cardboard and adhesive. Stiff coloured drawing paper can also be used to effect.

With a soldering iron a frame can be made out of metal, using string for the stays. The string can be strengthened by soaking it in glue first.

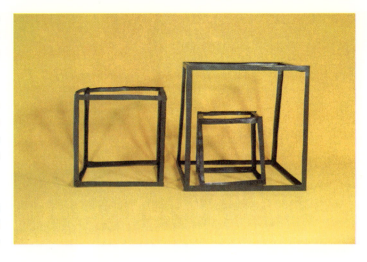

The basic frame can also be made of wood. Coloured threads could even be used as stays, thereby giving the impression of a loom.

The possibilities can be enlarged by using solid slabs—into which bars can be fitted—on one or two sides of the lattice.

Once again all sorts of different materials can be used; it doesn't have to be wood.

Besides the box-shaped lattice, there is also the spherical shape.

It can be seen that the spiral and the tube are closely related to each other.

If the spiral is wound tightly, the lattice structure becomes a tube with closed walls. As soon as the spiral is extended, it loses its tube-like character.

By joining the ends of the spiral together we can create a new form of complex spatial structure.

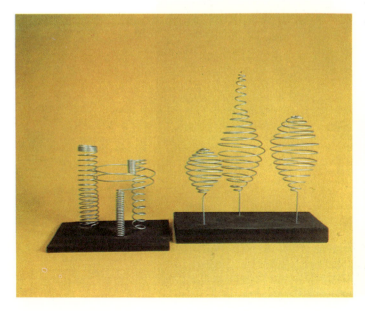

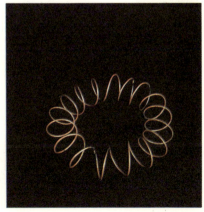

Building with hollow and latticed space

So far we have been dealing with particular types of individual spatial objects. This was necessary if we were to get a general picture of all the ideas and possibilities. But we do not really create anything until we start to build; only then are we concerned with proper spatial construction. Now we shall begin to see the full range of possibilities. It would be impossible to show all of them, but it is hoped that the illustrations will offer suggestions and act as stimuli for further creation.

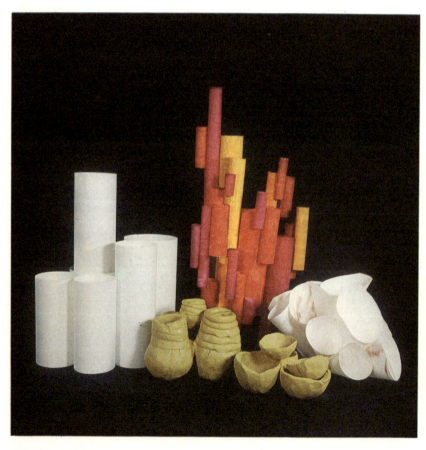

The same things apply to box constructions. Here the structural impression is even more striking. Box reliefs made of cardboard or clay, box combinations, and traversing box structures can be painted or glazed to make them even more effective.

Lattice constructions can also be combined and stacked together.

Clay bowls, tubes and containers are combined to make new structures, which then take on new functions. Such constructions can easily be made with clay, and the various parts can be put together without any visible joins. Sheet metal and cardboard are also suitable materials for this purpose.

Traversing shapes can be added to these 'combinations'.

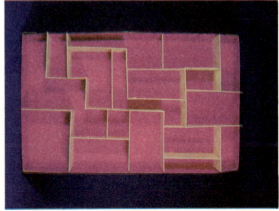

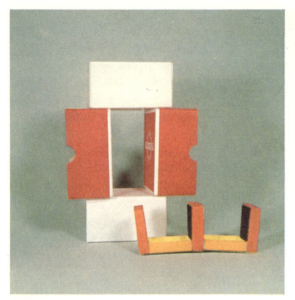

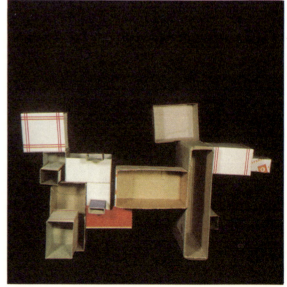

38

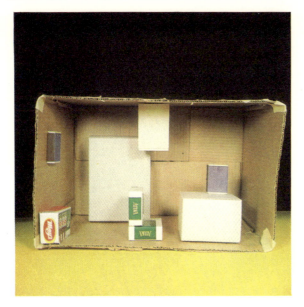

The doll's house is one type of box space with which even the smallest child is familiar. It can be used to illustrate the concepts of top, bottom, front and back. The illustration shows a basic structure which could easily be elaborated.

The most complex structures can be made of clay and then fired, though this depends, of course, on the quality, solidity, weight and quantity of the clay as well as the size of the kiln. But, in general, spatial objects made of folded cardboard are statically more reliable and technically easier to construct. The possibilities are endless. Large lattice constructions can, for example, be filled with smaller lattices.

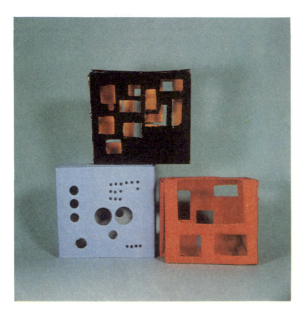

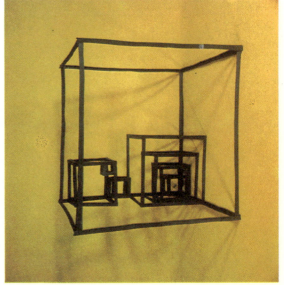

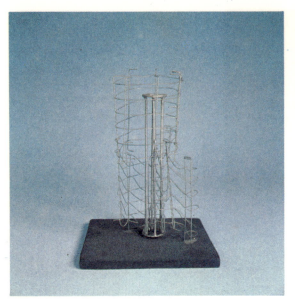
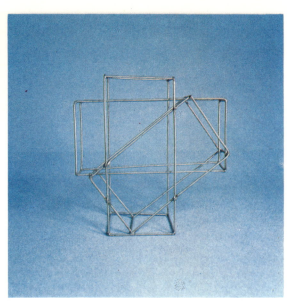

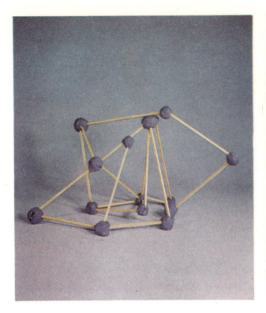
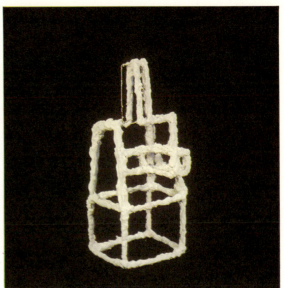

Many different shapes can be created with lattice constructions of wood or wire. Combined and traversing shapes are again possible.

But, as has been mentioned, we can really only give suggestions here. Many other constructions can be invented; and you do not have to stick rigidly to clay, wood or cardboard.

A latticed space can be constructed with little balls of modelling clay and straws or cocktail sticks.

Structures such as this are by no means permanent, of course.

Frames of binding wire can be strengthened with plaster of Paris. In order to do this, first build the frame, then soak soft paper (tissue paper or toilet paper) in plaster and wrap this round the wires. But some care is needed; it sounds much easier than it really is.

In fact, plaster of Paris is very useful in most types of spatial structure. It can be cut, scraped and, to a certain extent, even moulded.

The skeleton—traversed space

We can now move on to the creation and construction of 'spatial skeletons';

1. The 'spatial cross' with all its variations and combinations. With regard to materials the same applies as with the space lattice.

2. Spatial structures which, rather like a brush, have a single surface as their base and enclose space optically.

An individual rod does not express space; it penetrates space, but only indicates one dimension—length. As soon as we have two rods, however, a spatial area is indicated.

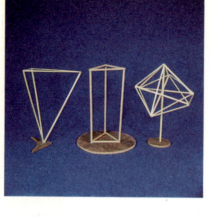

Three or more rods form a spatial frame.

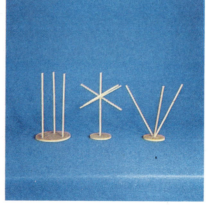

With the frame structure we can study the types of space covered by the 'skeleton'.

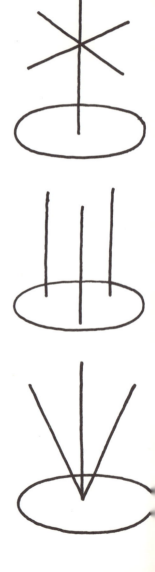

If we join the ends of the rods together, we create a type of scaffolding. In so doing we are immediately forming a type of space which has been discussed already and which we shall mention again later.

The 'brush principle' can be developed from its simplest form— three vertical rods. The closer the rods of the skeleton, the more distinct is the traversed space.

The same applies to the 'ray principle'. Here again a body is formed—right in the middle of surrounding space. There is no point where space is clearly demarcated.

Once again a large number of variations are possible.

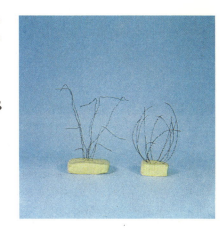

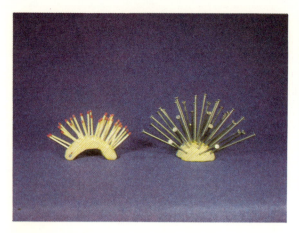

If the base is made of clay, it can then be curved or semispherical and form a foundation for totally new structures.

You can also use a spherical base, in which case the 'rays' reach out in all directions. In this way space crosses and ray spheres can be created.

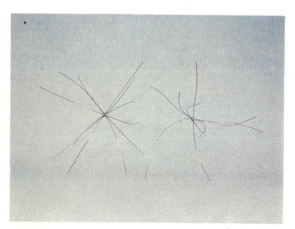

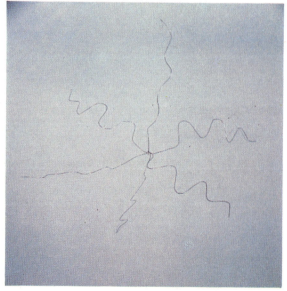

The 'cross' can also become something quite novel if its arms are shaped in various ways.

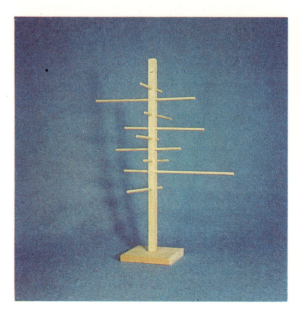

The space skeleton can be used for various constructions.

All sorts of things can be made with cocktail sticks, straws and branches.

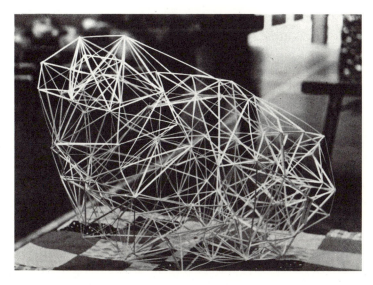

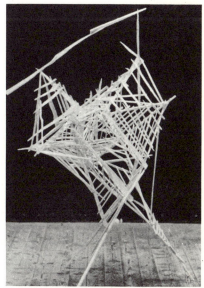

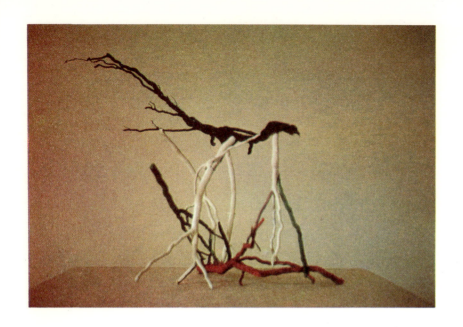

Wire can also be used. Thick wire should be soldered or brazed.

Intersections

Here we are concentrating on a particular form of the space skeleton which plays an important part in sculptural construction and can be exploited in many ways.

For this purpose glass, wood, clay, plaster of Paris, all sorts of sheet metal, acrylic or plexiglass, cardboard and corrugated paper are all ideal.

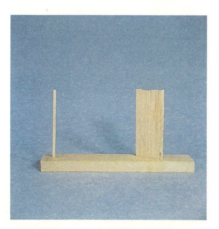

If we placed a number of rods next to each other they would form a partition—a partition extending into space. However, in order to save time and effort we might just as well use a flat surface as the partition.

We could, of course, easily join these surfaces together to make a box. But that is not the intention. We are more interested in an open construction containing these partitions or intersections.

The different elements can be joined together in various ways. Pieces of wood can be fitted together without glue by using a system of slots—as with many toy construction sets. These types of space skeleton have the advantage that they can always be reshaped. You could try the same thing with hard-baked clay slabs.

Cardboard and corrugated paper can also be cut and slotted together. It is advisable to strengthen larger objects with general-purpose adhesive. The basic structure can be enhanced by the use of colour. Corrugated paper and thin strips of wood (or rattan) are excellent for making surface frames.

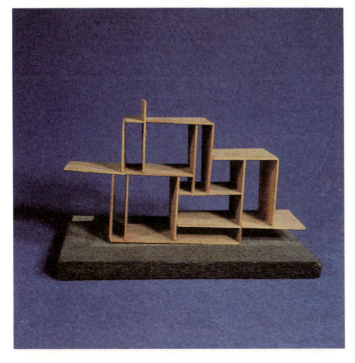

Glass can be cut with a glass cutter and joined together with general-purpose adhesive. Incidentally, there is no need to shy away from cutting glass; it is really quite easy.

Spatial compositions

So far we have concerned ourselves with individual spatial constructions and spatial objects
which could be used as parts of
larger structures.

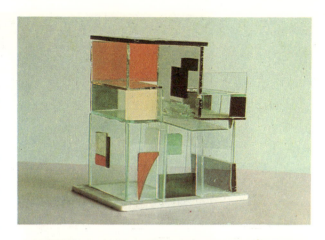

The next step is the co-ordination
of different types of space. This is
perhaps best illustrated by using
glass—cut and stuck with general-
purpose adhesive—as spaces
within spaces are then still visible.
(Note that for permanence special
glass adhesive should be used.)

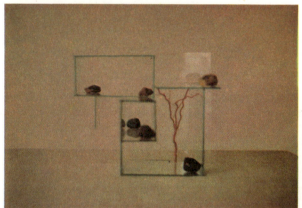

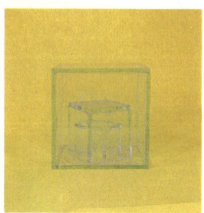

Spatial structures can be placed
and arranged within a large trans-
parent space. Yet another field for
discovery.

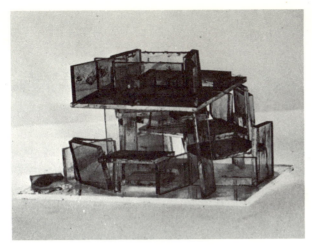

Then we come on to the 'space panorama', which provides the opportunity of combining all sorts of different shapes; in fact, all those with which we have been dealing.

This is rather like building a real house—erecting walls, using scaffolding, and so on.

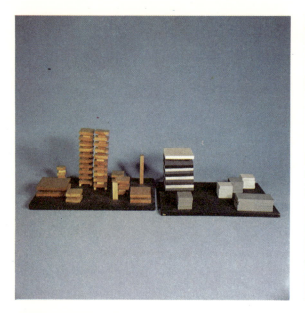

Real towns are planned in the same way—filled with blocks of apartments, towers, trees, television aerials and scaffolding. There are ideas and suggestions all around us if we only care to look.

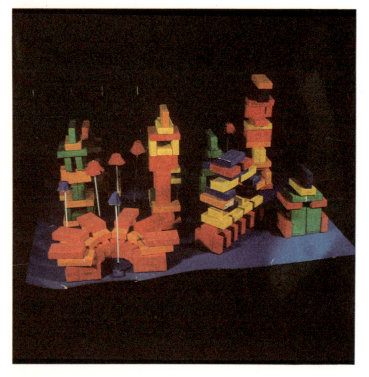

Representing space

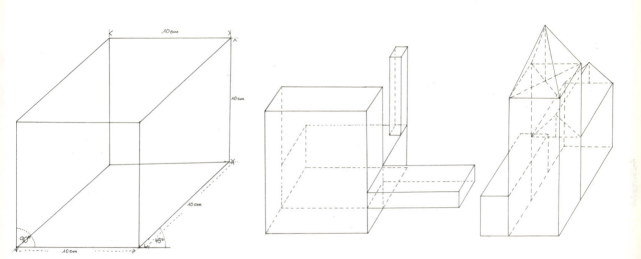

Isometric projection

There is a simple way of illustrating the principle of isometric projection. If you make two latticed spaces out of wire and carefully apply pressure to one of them, you will see that height and length remain the same in both lattices; only the interior and exterior angles change. An example is shown in the top left illustration, where the right angles are reduced to 45°.

Isometric projection falsifies spatial impressions in the sense that we are not used to seeing things in

53

this way. It is three-dimensional representation without perspective—a mathematical creation which can be made graphically more interesting by the use of colour.

Perspective

Our eyes are constantly playing tricks on us; from our standpoint it would seem that the nearest telegraph pole is taller than the next one and over twice as tall as those a bit further away. This phenomenon is the basis of pictorial perspective.

However, it is not our intention to go deeply into such a complex subject here; but in order to understand space fully, we need to have an idea of the basics of the perspective representation of space. The example with the telegraph poles serves well as a starting point.

To our eyes the telegraph poles eventually disappear on the horizon, and in this simple example there is only one vanishing point. But as soon as we deal with complex spatial structures, we find that there is more than one vanishing point. And everything is orientated towards a vanishing point. Parallels become distorted and this results in a spatial 'illu-

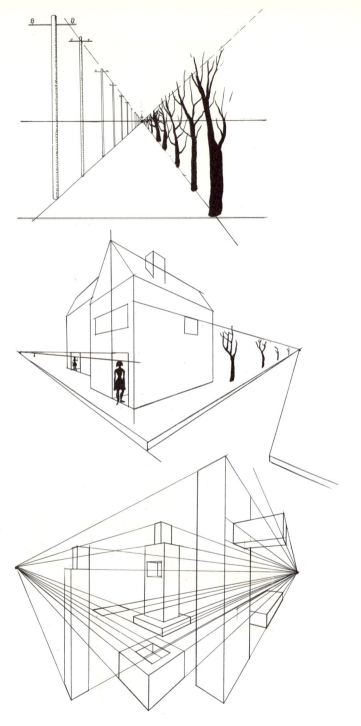

sion'. Perspective is a process of mathematical construction, not in itself an artistic phenomenon; pictorial design and composition simply make it so.

In this book we are interested in space and its representation and we shall not therefore go into the question of the perspective of houses, landscapes, etc., (With our system of two vanishing points we can represent anything we want to, including houses and landscapes. It is simply a question of fitting them into our system.)

The use of perspective is obviously of great pictorial interest in so far as it allows us to represent three-dimensional objects on a flat surface—that is, in two dimensions.

Understanding space

Three-dimensional thinking is the basis for three-dimensional design. You can only think in terms of space if you experience it at the same time, but such experience— seeing, touching, enclosing space —is in itself not enough to ensure a true knowledge and understanding of space. This can only be achieved by the actual creation of spatial structures.

A six-year-old child might well know his dog much better than anyone else, but this does not mean that he will not find it difficult to depict the dog 'spatially'—even to the point that it has two legs at the front and two at the back. If the child makes a model of the dog, however, and learns some of the peculiarities of space, he might well be able to understand fully what he 'knew' already.

This does not mean that the child will immediately transfer the knowledge gained from his sculptural experience into his drawings; he might well continue to draw in the same way for some time. He simply puts down his own ideas about that with which he has become familiar, and orders things according to his own laws.

But this child will have encountered space and has employed it actively. This is of great importance in that it helps to develop the child's powers of imagination. For this reason children should be given the opportunity—beginning with the first year at school—to make out of clay the things which they can draw or paint.

With three-dimensional objects it is possible for children to gain practical knowledge of the concepts of front, back, top, bottom, and so on.

The doll's house is a favourite with small children, and here a shoe box can be very useful (see page 39). And it need not necessarily be the well-known one-roomed house—more a theatre in which all sorts of inner and outer spaces can be represented.

Visualizing space has to be learned. The 'space around us' is full of instructive examples. Children should be encouraged to see and recognize all the different types of space in the world.

It is hoped that the illustrations in the Appendix will offer more suggestions on how to deal with space in a creative way.

Appendix—examples of pupils' and students' work.

Spatial structures made of small wooden blocks. The blocks were sawn from pieces of wood of various thicknesses, sandpapered and stuck together with general-purpose adhesive. They were then varnished with clear lacquer. (Boy, aged 12)

A cluster and a pile of glass splinters. Pieces of broken glass were wrapped in rags and smashed with a hammer. The splinters were then stuck together with adhesive. (Boy, aged 10)

An ordered chain of compact objects. (Student)

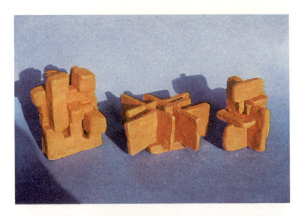

Spatial structures made of clay.

Clay vessels.

More clay structures.

Hollow body, made from plaster of Paris and then smoothed. The holes make possible a correspondence between inner and outer space. (Boy, aged 15)

Hollow spatial structure. This shows that hollow objects need not always be in the nature of 'vases'. (Student)

Cage structures in the shape of vintage cars. (Boy and girl, aged 10)

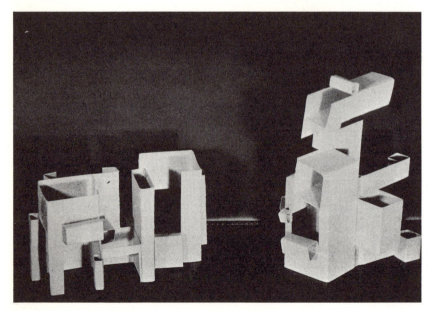

Strange spatial structures made with thick drawing paper. The various pieces were folded and slotted together, but not glued. (Boy, aged 12)

A right-angled spatial structure made of plastic-covered wire. (Student)

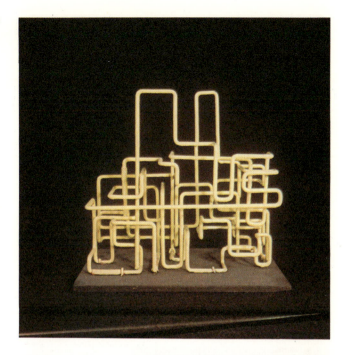

A tubular spatial structure.

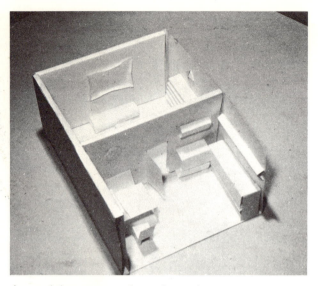

A column made of open wooden boxes. (Boy, aged 12)

A spatial structure, based on the doll's house, made of folded drawing paper. (Student)

The construction of a giant tower made with strips of folded paper. A good example of teamwork.

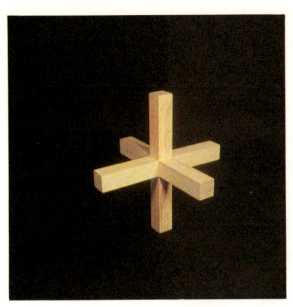

A spatial cross—carefully worked in wood. (Student)

Spatial structures made of rattan. (Girl, aged 13)

Strange structures made with strips of cardboard and based on the circle. (Boy, aged 9)

Loops made of thin strips of wood. (Student)

Wire structure. Groups of people, animals, houses, and so on, can be made in the same way. (Student)

A structure reaching out into space, inspired by the sight of a tree laden with fruit. (Boy, aged 9)

A perforated wall made of square blocks of wood which were polished and varnished. (Girl, aged 12)

A structure of spatial intersections, made of thin strips of wood stuck together. (Girl, aged 13)

A spiral reaching out into space
(based on the spiral staircase),
made of triangular pieces of wood.
(Boy, aged 14)

A relief wall made of three separate structures, which could also be used individually. (Student)

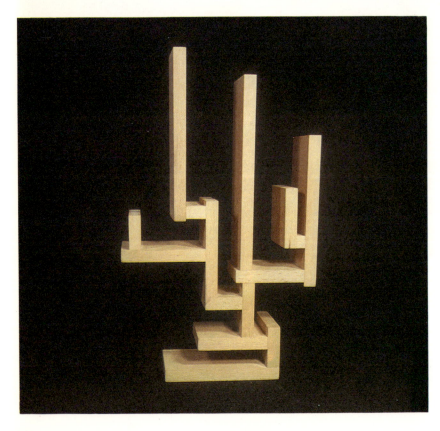

A wooden structure which forms an excellent example of the aesthetic effect to be gained from spatial objects. (Student)

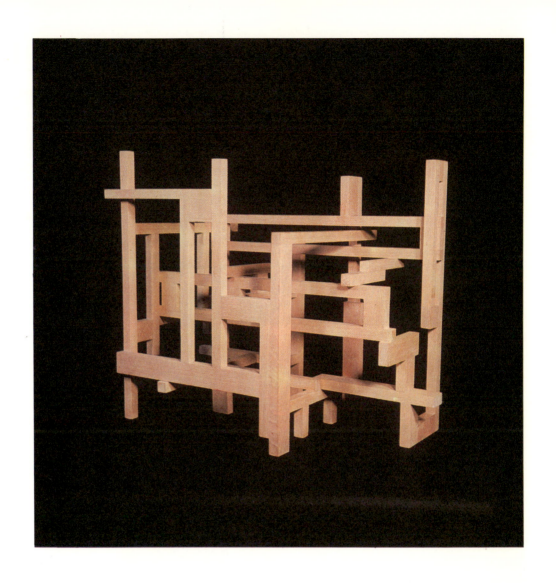

A spatial lattice which is also composed of interior lattices. Sandpapered wood stuck together. (Student)

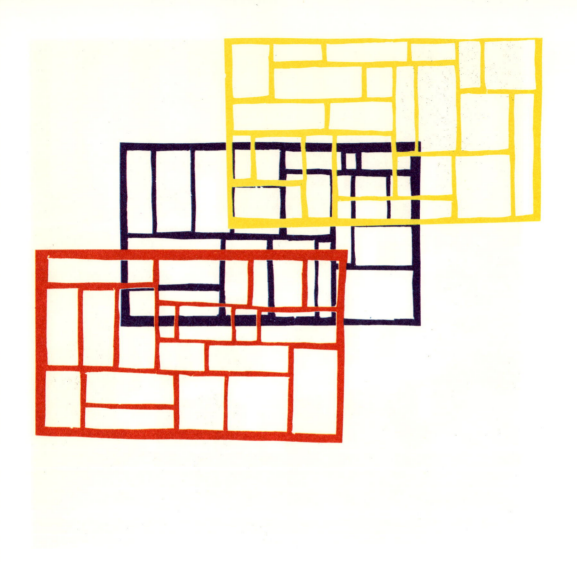

A spatial effect is gained by using
lattices of different colours. (Boy,
aged 12)

A spatial effect is gained in this collage by the use of perspective. (Girl, aged 12)

Table of Technical Skill Levels for Grades 1 through 12

One could become discouraged and assume that the subject of *Creating with Space and Construction* is only for older children, in fact only for young adults. But where should we begin to build up the knowledge about spacial relations in our world if not with the child? The purpose of this book is to provide food for thought and active inspiration for all ages. It is, of course, left up to each individual teacher to use the suggestions offered where he believes their application to be necessary and effective, based on the foundations prepared by him. The following table should only be taken as a general recommendation.

Grades 1 and 2:	4–6, 9, 10–15, 21, 22, 25, 34 top, 38, 41 top left, 43, 44, 46 top, 55, 67
Grades 2–4:	4–6, 7, 9, 10–20, 21–23, 25, 26, 28, 29, 30, 34 top, 38, 40 bottom right, 41 top left, 43, 44, 46 top, 48, 55, 62 top, 63 bottom, 64 bottom, 67
Grades 4 and 5:	4–6, 6–8, 9, 10–20, 21–23, 25, 26, 27, 28, 29, 30, 32, 34–35, 36, 37, 38, 39, 40 bottom right, 41, 43, 44, 45, 46, 47, 48, 49, 51, 55, 58, 62, 63 bottom, 64 bottom, 65 bottom, 67, 68, 69, 71
Grades 6 and 7:	4–6, 6–8, 9, 10–20, 21–23, 25, 26, 27, 28, 29, 30, 32, 33, 34–35, 36, 37, 38, 39, 40 bottom right, 41, 43, 44, 45, 46, 47, 48, 49, 50, 51, 52, 53, 54, 55, 58, 59, 62, 63, 64, 65, 66, 67, 68, 69, 70, 71, 72
Grades 8 and 9:	4–6, 6–8, 9, 10–20, 21–23, 25, 26, 27, 28, 29, 30, 32, 33, 34, 35, 36, 37, 38, 39, 40, 41, 42, 43, 44, 45, 46, 47, 48, 49, 50, 51, 52, 53, 54, 55, 58, 59, 60, 61, 62, 63, 64, 65, 66, 67, 68, 69, 70, 71, 72
Grades 10–12:	4–6, 6–8, 9, 10–20, 21, 23, 25, 26, 27, 28, 29, 30, 32, 33, 34–35, 36, 37, 38, 39, 40, 41, 42, 43, 44, 45, 46, 47, 48, 49, 50, 51, 52, 53, 54, 55, 58, 59, 60, 61, 62, 63, 64, 65, 66, 67, 68, 69, 70, 71, 72

Index